Numbers 1 to 5

Follow the arrows to see how each number is formed. Practise writing numbers and number words by following the dotted lines. Then write them without any help.

Numbers 6 to 10

Here are more numbers and number words for you to copy and practise.

6 66 six

7 77 seven

8 88 eight

9 99 nine

10 10 10 ten

Numbers 11 to 13

Trace the numbers and number words,
then write them on the lines underneath.

11   11

eleven

12   12

twelve

13   13

thirteen

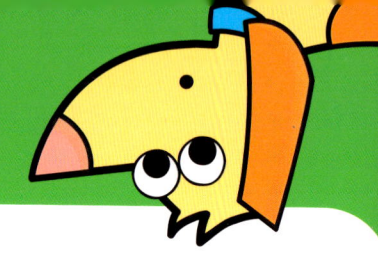

Numbers 14 to 20

Carry on practising writing numbers and number words.

14 14

fourteen

15 15

fifteen

16 16

sixteen

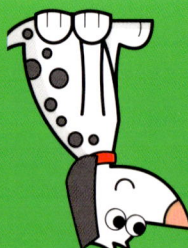

17 17

seventeen

18 18

eighteen

19 19

nineteen

20 20

twenty

Adding up

How good are you at adding up?
Find out by doing the addition
problems on this page and
the next.

1 + 1 = ☐   3 + 2 = ☐

4 + 3 = ☐   6 + 10 = ☐

5 + 1 = ☐   2 + 6 = ☐

2 + 8 = ☐   3 + 3 = ☐

2 + 1 = ☐   6 + 4 = ☐

2 + 2 = ☐   5 + 3 = ☐

4 + 2 = ☐   4 + 5 = ☐

10 + 4 = ☐   7 + 2 = ☐

8 + 2 = ☐   1 + 9 = ☐

2 + 3 = ☐   4 + 4 = ☐

1 + 5 = ☐   10 + 7 = ☐

2 + 7 = ☐   5 + 2 = ☐

4 + 1 = ☐   7 + 3 = ☐

3 + 4 = ☐   3 + 6 = ☐

10 + 8 = ☐   2 + 4 = ☐

3 + 5 = ☐   10 + 2 = ☐

5 + 5 = ☐   3 + 7 = ☐

8 + 1 = ☐   1 + 7 = ☐

6 + 2 = ☐   4 + 6 = ☐

2 + 5 = ☐   1 + 3 = ☐

Taking away

Now try the taking away
problems on this page and the next.

10 – 1 = ☐   8 – 7 = ☐

6 – 3 = ☐   5 – 4 = ☐

4 – 4 = ☐   3 – 2 = ☐

1 – 1 = ☐   7 – 5 = ☐

5 – 1 = ☐   9 – 6 = ☐

9 – 8 = ☐   9 – 4 = ☐

7 – 4 = ☐   6 – 6 = ☐

5 – 2 = ☐   2 – 2 = ☐

$10 - 4 =$ ☐ $8 - 5 =$ ☐

$6 - 4 =$ ☐ $10 - 9 =$ ☐

$8 - 8 =$ ☐ $7 - 3 =$ ☐

$5 - 3 =$ ☐ $10 - 8 =$ ☐

$7 - 6 =$ ☐ $5 - 1 =$ ☐

$5 - 5 =$ ☐ $7 - 7 =$ ☐

$8 - 3 =$ ☐ $6 - 2 =$ ☐

$7 - 3 =$ ☐ $9 - 2 =$ ☐

$4 - 2 =$ ☐ $6 - 5 =$ ☐

$2 - 1 =$ ☐ $8 - 6 =$ ☐

$10 - 3 =$ ☐ $9 - 6 =$ ☐

$8 - 1 =$ ☐ $10 - 5 =$ ☐

Number patterns

Can you spot which numbers are missing?

1 _ 3 _ 5 _

6 7 _ _ 10

2 _ 4 _ 6 _ 8

1 _ 3 _ 5 _ 7

10 _ 8 _ 6 _

5 _ 3 _ 1

2 _ 6 _ 10

1 3 _ 7 _

2 _ 4 _ 6 _ 8 _

1 _ 3 _ 5 _ 7 _

1 _ 3 4 _ 4 3 _ _

10 _ 8 _ 8 9 _

2 2 _ 3 _ 4

5 5 5 5 _ 4 4 4
_ 3 3 3 2 _ _ 2

More adding up

Here are some more adding problems for you to try.

11 + 1 = ☐   13 + 2 = ☐

11 + 9 = ☐   14 + 3 = ☐

11 + 5 = ☐   12 + 6 = ☐

17 + 1 = ☐   16 + 3 = ☐

12 + 4 = ☐   11 + 2 = ☐

14 + 4 = ☐   13 + 5 = ☐

12 + 1 = ☐   11 + 4 = ☐

14 + 2 = ☐   11 + 8 = ☐

$12 + 3 = \boxed{}$ $16 + 4 = \boxed{}$

$13 + 1 = \boxed{}$ $17 + 2 = \boxed{}$

$16 + 3 = \boxed{}$ $13 + 6 = \boxed{}$

$12 + 8 = \boxed{}$ $13 + 4 = \boxed{}$

$15 + 1 = \boxed{}$ $12 + 2 = \boxed{}$

$12 + 6 = \boxed{}$ $13 + 7 = \boxed{}$

$15 + 4 = \boxed{}$ $16 + 1 = \boxed{}$

$14 + 5 = \boxed{}$ $14 + 6 = \boxed{}$

$12 + 5 = \boxed{}$ $11 + 3 = \boxed{}$

$19 + 1 = \boxed{}$ $15 + 2 = \boxed{}$

$13 + 3 = \boxed{}$ $11 + 7 = \boxed{}$

$18 + 1 = \boxed{}$ $15 + 3 = \boxed{}$

More taking away

Try the taking away problems on this page and the next.

20 − 1 = ☐ 19 − 4 = ☐

18 − 8 = ☐ 17 − 1 = ☐

16 − 5 = ☐ 11 − 1 = ☐

20 − 7 = ☐ 19 − 2 = ☐

18 − 4 = ☐ 17 − 7 = ☐

14 − 4 = ☐ 12 − 1 = ☐

20 − 3 = ☐ 17 − 4 = ☐

15 − 5 = ☐ 13 − 1 = ☐

12 − 2 = ☐   19 − 1 = ☐

16 − 3 = ☐   20 − 5 = ☐

15 − 4 = ☐   19 − 8 = ☐

15 − 2 = ☐   19 − 5 = ☐

18 − 7 = ☐   17 − 5 = ☐

16 − 6 = ☐   15 − 3 = ☐

13 − 2 = ☐   18 − 1 = ☐

19 − 3 = ☐   20 − 8 = ☐

17 − 3 = ☐   14 − 1 = ☐

20 − 2 = ☐   13 − 3 = ☐

19 − 6 = ☐   20 − 4 = ☐

18 − 6 = ☐   17 − 2 = ☐

More number patterns

Using numbers between 1 and 30, complete the number patterns on this page and the next.

3 _ 9 _ 15 _

4 _ 12 _ 20 _

20 _ _ 17 _ _ 15

5 _ 15 _ 25 _

_ 17 _ 19 20 _

11 _ 13 _ 15 _

_ 6 _ 10 _ 14 _

2 _ 4 4 _ 6 8 _

10 _ 14 _ 18 _

3 6 9 _ 9 6 3

20 _ 16 _ 12

1 3 _ 7 9 _

20 17 _ 11 8 _

20 16 _ 8 _

1 5 9 _ 17

Adding up and taking away

Try the adding up and taking away problems
on this page and the next.

11 + 1 = ☐   20 – 15 = ☐

13 + 4 = ☐   18 – 5 = ☐

12 + 1 = ☐   17 – 11 = ☐

11 + 8 = ☐   20 – 20 = ☐

1 + 9 = ☐   18 – 12 = ☐

12 + 8 = ☐   19 – 3 = ☐

13 + 5 = ☐   18 – 17 = ☐

8 + 11 = ☐   15 – 5 = ☐

$9 + 9 =$ ⬚ $20 - 8 =$ ⬚

$3 + 10 =$ ⬚ $20 - 13 =$ ⬚

$16 + 4 =$ ⬚ $18 - 8 =$ ⬚

$4 + 11 =$ ⬚ $19 - 1 =$ ⬚

$13 + 1 =$ ⬚ $16 - 11 =$ ⬚

$17 + 2 =$ ⬚ $15 - 2 =$ ⬚

$14 + 5 =$ ⬚ $10 - 9 =$ ⬚

$11 + 8 =$ ⬚ $20 - 7 =$ ⬚

$8 + 8 =$ ⬚ $17 - 1 =$ ⬚

$1 + 13 =$ ⬚ $18 - 8 =$ ⬚

$15 + 3 =$ ⬚ $20 - 8 =$ ⬚

$13 + 7 =$ ⬚ $15 - 9 =$ ⬚

Numbers 21 to 60

Trace each number, then practise
writing them on the lines.

21 22 23 24 25

26 27 28 29 30

31 32 33 34 35

36 37 38 39 40

41 42 43 44 45

46 47 48 49 50

51 52 53 54 55

56 57 58 59 60